HOW THEY LIVED

A SAXON FARMER

STEWART ROSS

Illustrated by
Mark Bergin

HOW THEY LIVED

An American Pioneer Family
A Crusading Knight
A Family in World War II
An Ice Age Hunter
A Medieval Serf
A Plantation Slave
A Roman Centurion
A Saxon Farmer
A Victorian Factory Worker

First Published in 1985 by
Wayland (Publishers) Limited
49 Lansdowne Place, Hove
East Sussex BN3 1HF, England

British Library Cataloguing in Publication Data
Ross, Stewart
A Saxon Farmer — (How they lived)
1. Country life — England — Juvenile literature
2. England — Social life and customs — to 1066
— Juvenile literature
I. Title.   II. Bergin, Mark   III. Series
942' .009'734   DA152.2

ISBN 0 85078 562 6

Typeset by Planagraphic Typesetters Limited
Printed in Italy by G. Canale & C.S.p.A., Turin
Bound in Great Britain by The Bath Press, Avon

CONTENTS

A STURDY WORKER

The farmer stood and looked at his day's work. Ten trees felled. At this rate he would be finished before the end of the winter. He glanced up at the darkening sky. It was going to rain. He had better get home before he got wet.

The fair-haired man swung his axe over his shoulder. Steadily he walked along the muddy path. A few lights twinkled ahead of him, and he hurried towards them. There were wolves in the forest in which he had been working.

Anglo-Saxon farmers did much to make the landscape as we know it today. After the Romans had left England in the fifth century, their system of law and order soon broke down. Foreigners invaded the country

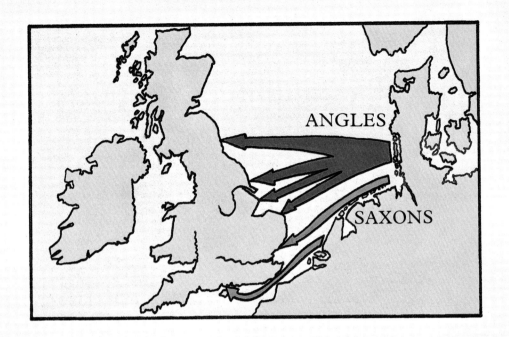

ANGLES

SAXONS

and conquered it. The two main groups of invaders were Angles and Saxons. They came from Holland, Germany and Denmark. The Saxons took most of southern England.

Gradually the Saxons settled down. They grew to like the land they had taken. They founded villages and

The Angles and the Saxons sailed across the North Sea to Britain.

cleared new fields, as the man described above was doing. By the eighth century they had built up a strong civilization. A few of them lived in towns and traded widely. But most of the Saxons and their families were farmers.

CLEARING THE LAND

A Saxon axehead.

There were not many people living in England in the fifth century. Saxon farmers had plenty of land on which to work but not much of it was suitable for farming. East Anglia, for example, was too marshy. Other land was hard and stony, with thin soil. The moors were like this. Much of the rest of the country was covered with huge forests.

The Saxons were keen to open up new fields. The trees of the forests were massive oaks, beeches and ash. Slowly they were cut down and burned. The huge stumps left in the ground often took years to remove. However, by the eleventh century, England was starting to look as it does today.

Place names tell us where the Saxon farmers settled. Sometimes a group of families followed a leader. The Saxon word 'ing', means 'followers of'. So Hastings was where the followers of Haesta settled. The endings 'ley' and 'hurst' mean clearings in the forest. Penshurst was Pefen's clearing.

A few farmers built their homes far from other houses. This was dangerous. Most farmers preferred living in groups. Any place ending in 'ham' or 'ton' was once an Anglo-Saxon village. Can you guess what we call the place where Beornmund's people settled? It's Birmingham.

The Saxons cut down large areas of woodland to clear new fields.

7

LIFE ON THE FARM

In most of southern England Saxon farmers shared fields. Each had some strips of land in large common fields. In Kent, East Anglia and Devon, families owned the land around their house, and they had labourers (often slaves) to help them.

The Saxons invaded England in fighting bands, led by a lord. When they became farmers they kept their lords. They had to help their lords by paying them money, or by working on their farms.

The farmer and his family were kept busy all the year round. The hus-

Saxon farmers grew peas, beans, lentils, cereals and fruit.

band did the ploughing, the ditching and other heavy work. Wives and children helped with sowing and harvesting. They also did the milking and brewing. There was always work to be done on the farm, except in the middle of winter.

Saxon farmers grew everything they could. The most popular crop was barley. The Anglo-Saxon word for barley was 'bere'. The place where it was stored was a 'bere-aern', from which we get the English word barn. Farmers grew wheat, fruit, and vines for wine. They also kept chickens, goats, pigs, sheep, cattle and plenty of bees. There was no sugar in Saxon times, so honey was important to sweeten food.

The Saxons kept bees for honey which they used to sweeten food. They also made a drink, called mead, from honey.

THE VILLAGE

The Saxons were the people who first built villages in England. In the early days farmers grouped their houses tightly together round a green or a well. Often they built a fence round the village to protect it from wolves or their enemies. Later villages became more spread out. Sometimes they grew up beside a road. Other villages were more higgledy-piggledy, just several farms near each other.

Before the seventh century, the biggest building in the village was the lord's hall. This was like a huge wooden barn with a thatched roof. The villagers met there for feasts. Churches were built when the Saxons became Christian. Most Saxon churches were wooden, but a few stone ones are still standing today. The church was certainly the largest building in the village.

Although Saxon farmers were skilled at many jobs, they couldn't

Many Saxon settlements were the foundations of today's villages and towns.

do everything themselves. Craftsmen lived in the villages, along with the farmers. The miller lived in his mill beside a river or stream. He ground the farmers' corn into flour. Other important men were the village blacksmith and the carpenter. There were weavers and potters, too, and large villages probably had a tanner. He prepared the skins of animals for making into clothing. In his village the Saxon farmer could find everything he needed for his simple life.

Most villages had a blacksmith. This carving shows the mythical Wayland Smith at work.

AT HOME

Saxon farmers enjoyed the summer. They had to work hard to harvest their crops but the days were warm and there was plenty of food. There was beef, mutton and pork to eat, and they hunted venison and other game in the forests. The rivers and sea were full of fish. Orchards gave fruit, and eggs, bread and butter were produced on the farm.

In the winter the story was different. They sat for long dark hours huddled in their cold huts. Most of the farm animals were killed in the autumn, because there wasn't enough food to keep them through the winter.

Hunting was more a pastime of wealthy Saxons but many farmers probably hunted too.

There were no dentists or doctors in Saxon times. The man on the right has had a tooth pulled out with a pair of pliers.

The farmer and his family chewed on dried or salted meat. They had no other way to preserve food.

Although he was sometimes short of food, the Saxon farmer always had enough to drink. Streams and wells provided clean water and cows and goats gave milk. Everyone in the family drank wine, ale and sweet mead, a drink made from honey.

The farmers lived outdoor lives, but they were not very healthy. They did not understand medicine or hygiene. Babies often died before they reached one year old. Wounds went septic, aching teeth were pulled out with pliers, and broken bones often healed crookedly. The Saxons had to be tough to survive.

CLOTHES AND SHELTER

Most Saxon women had to make clothes for themselves and their families. Farmers' wives wore long dresses, called tunics, and sandals. Tunics were made of wool. They were dyed simple bright colours, and the edges were embroidered. Women also covered their heads with hoods.

Saxon men wore thick woollen trousers and short tunics. Their shoes were fastened by long leather straps that were tied criss-cross up their legs. A farmer always carried a dagger, in case of danger. When at work in the fields he wore a heavy cape to keep out the wind and rain.

Farm houses were small and simple. Poorer farmers had round houses, like wigwams. The walls were made of mud and sticks, and the roof was thatched. Wealthier farmers built larger houses of wooden planks.

Houses had no chimneys or glass windows, so the inside of a farmer's house was dark and smoky. A poor farmer kept his cattle under the same roof, divided by a hurdle from the room where his family lived. A fire burned in the middle of the floor, for

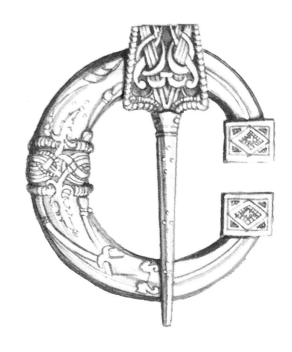

Above *A brooch like this one would have been used to fasten a Saxon's cloak.*

Right *Saxon clothes were made from woven sheep's wool. Flax was also grown to make a finer cloth called linen.*

warmth and cooking. Larger houses usually had a table and a couple of benches, but no beds. Everyone slept on the floor.

FEASTS AND POEMS

The Saxons kept some customs from their days as soldiers. They liked to gather together and sing or listen to stories from the past. In the summer months they were too busy for anything but work. The winter was the season of feasts and poems.

Some Saxon feasts, like the Yule feast in December, were enjoyed by the whole village. Others were only for

the men. On special evenings they met in the hall of their lord. Here they ate and drank heartily. Then the dishes were cleared and the entertainment began. Musicians played the harp and sang, others joined in the

Above *Saxons drank from leather cups waterproofed with animal fat. Wealthy Saxons had beautifully carved drinking horns.*

chorus, thumping the rhythm on the rough tables. Women were hardly mentioned in the songs and poems which told of past victories and heroes. When the men were in the hall, women stayed at home, or prepared the food.

As the evening drew on and the fire burned lower, the time came for an epic poem. A hush settled on the hall. The poet stood, and began to recite:

Listen! We know about the glory of kings long ago . . .

The poem was *Beowulf,* the story of a warrior and his struggle against monsters. At the end, the hero was bitten in the neck by a dragon and died. Other stories told of battles and brave deeds. The farmers loved them.

Above *A Saxon harp.*

Left *A lot of wine, ale and mead was drunk at a Saxon feast.*

KINGDOMS, SHIRES, AND THE LAW

Saxon kings arranged their people into hundreds. This was a group of one hundred families, with a 'hundred man' in charge. He collected the farmers' taxes. He also organized the local law court, which often met on a hill near the village.

A farmer accused of a crime had to swear in court that he was innocent. For serious crimes, he had to find men to swear with him. They were called oath-helpers. If he couldn't find enough oath-helpers, he faced an ordeal.

In the ordeal by iron, the accused man had to walk nine feet (about three metres) holding a piece of red hot iron in his hand. If his hand was healing well after three days, this was a sign from the Gods that he was innocent. Guilty men faced horrible

Like our courts today, Saxon courts decided the punishment for a crime.

The ordeal by iron was a very painful way of proving a person's innocence.

punishments like prison, fines, flogging, mutilation or execution. Every man, woman and child had their price, called their wergild. If a man killed a farmer in Kent, he had to pay the victim's family 200 shillings.

The hundreds were gathered into shires, like Hampshire. Each shire had its own court and head man, called an ealdorman. The Saxon far-mer also belonged to a kingdom, made up of several shires. The names of many of these kingdoms are still with us today. The south Saxons, for example, formed the Kingdom of Sussex.

In Saxon times there was no paper money. These are reproductions of Saxon coins.

19

PAGAN GODS

The Saxon farmers who first came to England brought their beliefs with them. They believed in many gods. Each god had different powers and the Saxons devoted separate days of the week to worshipping them. Tiw was a god of war and death and his name is remembered in Tuesday. Thursday was Thor's day, he was a god of thunder and lightning. The most powerful god was Woden. His name is found in Wednesday.

When a farmer was buried, gifts were buried with him. These were presents for the grave gods. They were also useful objects for a life after death. Men had tools, cups and weapons beside them in the grave. Some even had their wives or slaves buried with them.

Poor Saxon farmers probably buried their dead in wooden boxes. Wealthier Saxons were cremated when they died, and their ashes were put into decorated pottery urns.

Near his village the Saxon farmer had a special place for worship. Sometimes this was a hill top, or a clearing in the woods. Here priests and priestesses lived in dark huts, and farmers made sacrifices before weird carved idols. This was done to keep the gods happy.

Saxon farmers had little education. Magic was important to them. They wore rings to protect them from

Before the Saxons became Christian their pagan priest told them how to make sacrifices to please their gods.

danger. Children were left on the roofs of houses to be cured of fever. Saxons believed in dragons, demons and elves. Drakelow, in Derbyshire, meant 'Dragon mount'. No Saxon dared go out alone at night near that frightening spot.

CHRISTIANITY

Saxon farmers learned about Christianity from the preaching of monks. The new faith spread slowly west from Kent in the seventh century. Missionaries sent from Rome and Ireland first won the support of a local king. Then, when they arrived in a village, they pulled down the old idols. A huge cross was put up in their place.

The farmers gathered from miles around to see what was happening. Occasionally, if they were angry at what the monks were doing, they killed them. More often they listened to the Christian gospel with interest. The new religion appealed strongly to the Saxons. Sometimes hundreds were baptized in a nearby river in one day.

At first all services were outside, in the holy places. After a time villagers joined together to build their own church. The lord gave most of the money and the farmers took it in turns to help with the work. Early churches were wooden, but by the tenth century some stone ones were being built.

Church services were in Latin which the farmers didn't understand. Their faith was simple, and mixed with magic. But Christianity was important to them. They gave one tenth of all their produce to the priest. This was all he earned.

Before churches were built, Saxons newly converted to Christianity erected stone crosses and worshipped in the open air.

Greenstead Church in Essex is one of the oldest Saxon churches in England.

THE ANGLO-SAXON LANGUAGE

The language of the Saxon farmers was different from our own. They spoke Anglo-Saxon. Modern English has grown out of Anglo-Saxon, and some of the words we use are like those used by the Saxon farmers. Most of our farming and countryside words come from Anglo-Saxon. The words are short and simple. A few examples are shown on this page.

Very few farmers learned to read and write. This is what written Anglo-Saxon looks like:

Although written Anglo-Saxon looks strange to us, some Anglo-Saxon words are very similar to the English ones we use today.

ᚻ ᚠᚾ ᚩᚦᚫᛚ ᚠᚱᚪᚾ ᚳᚣᛗᚾᚷ ᚠᛖ ᛈ ᛚ ᚪᚩᚱᚾᚻᚫᚠᚾ.

This is the first line of a poem called The Battle of Banburgh. It reads:

In this year king Athelstan,
lord of the warriors . . .

Feld (Field)

Kye (Cow)

Treow (Tree)

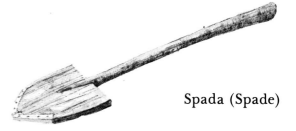

Spada (Spade)

The handwriting is very strange to us. The Anglo-Saxon alphabet had some letters that we don't have. The sign Þ, for example, was a th. No wonder Anglo-Saxon is hard to read.

A beautifully illustrated page from the Lindisfarne Gospels which was written in Latin by monks. The hand-written Anglo-Saxon translation can also be seen.

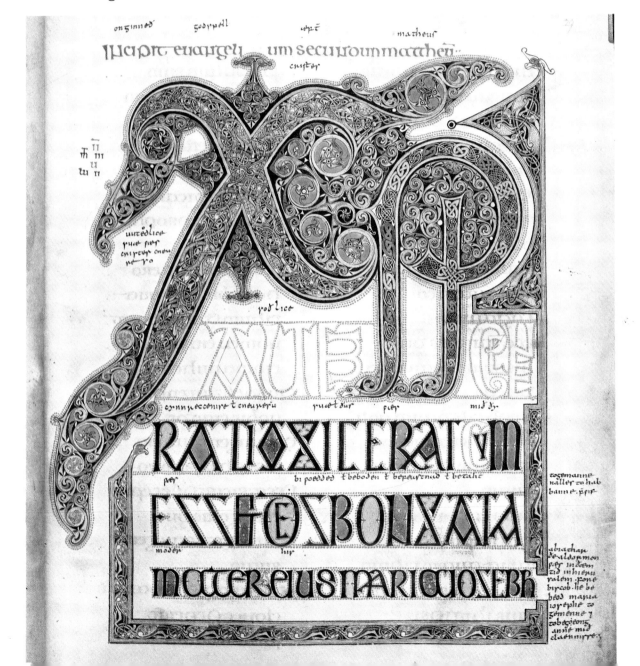

THE CALL-UP

The Saxons first came to England as soldiers. Farmers were never allowed to forget this. At any time, when danger threatened, the king could order them to join his army. This army of part-time soldiers was known as the fyrd.

In early Saxon days each farmer kept a spear, a sword and a shield at home. These were all the weapons he needed. As time went on, however, a soldier's needs became more complicated. King Alfred of Wessex, who reigned between the years 871 and 899, wanted men with chain-mail armour, helmets, battle-axes and, if possible, horses. The ordinary farmer couldn't afford to buy these for all his men, so a new law was made. This said that, instead of every man having to fight, a farmer had to send only two men for each plough he owned.

If a man failed to turn up when the king called for him, he could be fined £5. This was a vast sum of money in those days. Worse still, if he left the army to go home without permission, he could be executed.

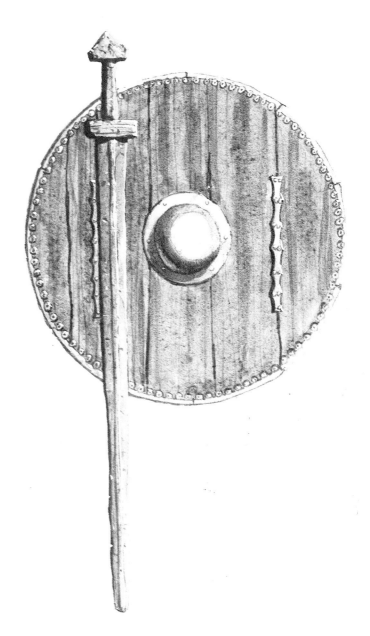

Left *A Saxon farmer could be called to join the king's army at any time.*

Right *A Saxon sword and shield.*

INVADERS

For almost three hundred years Saxon farmers lived fairly peacefully in southern England. Gradually, they cleared the land and expanded their farms. Villages grew and trade flourished. Christianity spread amongst them. Then the Vikings came.

In 782 three long ships were sighted near Portland in Dorset. Fierce looking men came ashore. Beorhtric, king of Wessex, sent a messenger to ask the foreigners who they were. The Vikings killed the royal servant and destroyed several farms. Then they climbed back into their ships and sailed away.

From this time onwards, the farmers of southern England never knew when they might be attacked again. The Vikings came from the cold countries of northern Europe. They were determined to conquer the Saxons and make England their own. Men who had farms near the coast, or beside rivers, carried weapons with them at all times. Fortified towns,

Saxons who lived by the sea learned to look out for the ships of invading Vikings.

called burghs, were built. Farmers had to be ready to join the fyrd at a moment's notice.

In 865 a large Viking army invaded southern England. It remained for over 150 years and many battles were fought as the Saxons struggled to keep their land. Sometimes the Saxons won, at other times the Vikings were victorious. Many farmers and their families were killed and their farms were burned to the ground. Finally, in 1016, a Viking king called Cnut ruled all England.

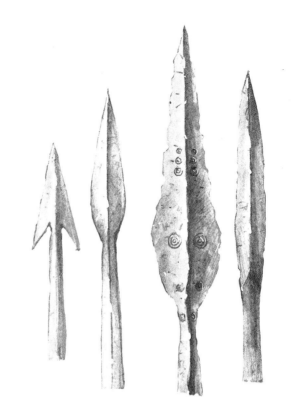

Some spearheads of the Saxon period.

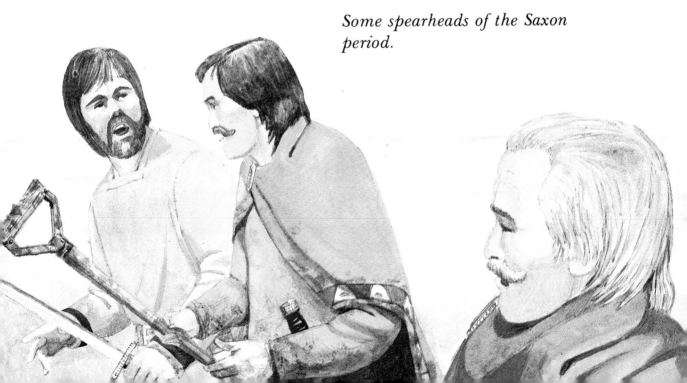

THE END OF SAXON ENGLAND

The Saxon farmers' lives did not change much when Cnut became king. They kept the same lords, and they farmed as they had always done. But a much greater change was soon to come.

In 1066 a Saxon king, Harold, again ruled England, but his reign did not last long. In September he defeated invaders in the north. Then he hurried south to face a more dangerous enemy — the Normans.

The fyrd gathered for the last time. On 14th October they were beaten in a bloody battle near Hastings. The Normans then went on to conquer all England, and the Saxon farmers lost their land to new masters. In a few years their way of life had vanished.

The Bayeux Tapestry tells the story of the Battle of Hastings which took place in 1066, and marked the end of Saxon England.

GLOSSARY

Chain-mail Armour made from iron rings.

Civilization An organized way of life.

Epic A long story.

Idol A statue of a god.

Landscape The shape and layout of the countryside.

Latin The language of the ancient Romans.

Missionary One who tries to spread his faith to other countries.

Monk A man who gives his whole life to God.

Mutilate To cut off part of a body.

Venison The meat of deer.

MORE BOOKS TO READ

John Hamilton, *Saxon England* (Lutterworth Press, 1964)

David Jones, *Your Book of Anglo-Saxon England* (Faber and Faber, 1970)

Robin May, *Alfred the Great and the Saxons* (Wayland, 1984)

Amanda Purves, *Growing Up in a Saxon Village* (Wayland, 1978)

Tony Triggs, *The Saxons* (Macdonald Educational, 1979)

INDEX

Picture acknowledgements

The pictures in this book were supplied by the following: the Bodleian Library, Oxford, 9; Courtesy of the Trustees of the British Museum, 25; British Tourist Authority, 23. The remaining pictures are from the Wayland Picture Library.